Pebble® Plus

Earth in Action

Tornadoes

by Mari Schuh

Consulting Editor: Gail Saunders-Smith, PhD

Consultant: Susan L. Cutter, PhD
Carolina Distinguished Professor and Director,
Hazards & Vulnerability Research Institute
Department of Geography, University of South Carolina

Capstone
press®

Mankato, Minnesota

Pebble Plus is published by Capstone Press,
151 Good Counsel Drive, P.O. Box 669, Mankato, Minnesota 56002.
www.capstonepress.com

 Books published by Capstone Press are manufactured with paper
containing at least 10 percent post-consumer waste.

Library of Congress Cataloging-in-Publication Data
Schuh, Mari, 1975–
    Tornadoes / by Mari Schuh.
    p. cm. — (Pebble Plus. Earth in action)
    Summary: "Describes tornadoes, how they form, and the tools scientists use to predict them" — Provided by
publisher.
    Includes bibliographical references and index.
    ISBN 978-1-4296-3434-2 (lib. bdg.)
    1. Tornadoes — Juvenile literature. I. Title. II. Series.
QC955.2.S38 2010
551.55'3 — dc22   2009002174

Editorial Credits
Erika L. Shores, editor; Lori Bye, designer; Wanda Winch, media researcher

Photo Credits
AP Images/Lori Mehmen, 11
Capstone Press/Karon Dubke, 15, 17
Compass Point Books/Lori Bye, 6
FEMA News Photo/Jocelyn Augustino, 21
Getty Images Inc./America 24-7/Kyle Gerstner, 7; Science Faction/Jim Reed, 13
iStockphoto/Andreas Prott, 9; David Claassen, 19
Peter Arnold/Gene & Karen Rhoden, 1, 5; Gene Rhoden, cover

**The author dedicates this book to the Field Station volunteers at Kenosha Public Museum
    in Kenosha, Wisconsin.**

Note to Parents and Teachers

The Earth in Action set supports national science standards related to earth science. This
book describes and illustrates tornadoes. The images support early readers in understanding
the text. The repetition of words and phrases helps early readers learn new words. This book
also introduces early readers to subject-specific vocabulary words, which are defined in the
Glossary section. Early readers may need assistance to read some words and to use the Table of
Contents, Glossary, Read More, Internet Sites, and Index sections of the book.

122009
005650R

Table of Contents

What Is a Tornado?

Tornadoes are

very strong windstorms.

These swirling funnels

race across the land.

Where Tornadoes Form

Tornadoes happen worldwide.

The central United States has

hundreds of tornadoes a year.

People call it Tornado Alley.

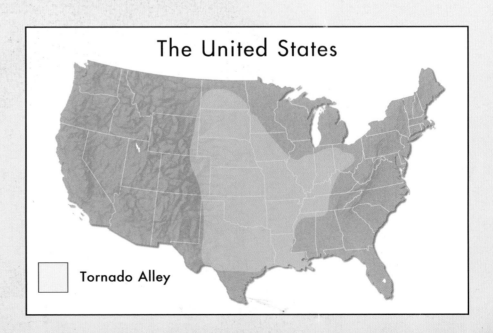

The United States

Tornado Alley

How Tornadoes Form

Most tornadoes happen
in spring and summer.
They form from big thunderstorms.

9

During some storms, warm and cold air masses meet. Wind spins the air into a funnel cloud. If the spinning cloud reaches the ground, it is a tornado.

Staying Safe

Meteorologists use Doppler radar to watch for tornadoes. Trained people also help spot tornadoes outside.

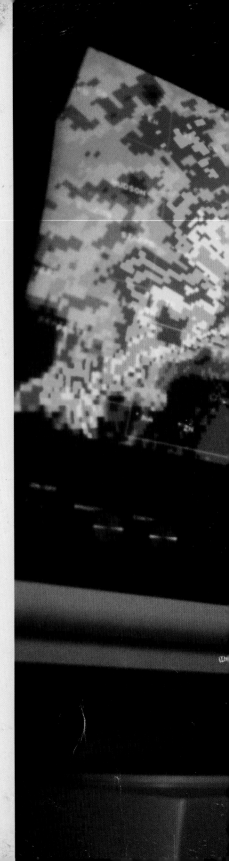

Outside, listen for storm sirens.

Inside, listen to the radio or

watch TV for storm warnings.

Go to a basement

or a windowless room

to stay safe.

If you're outside,

lie down in a ditch.

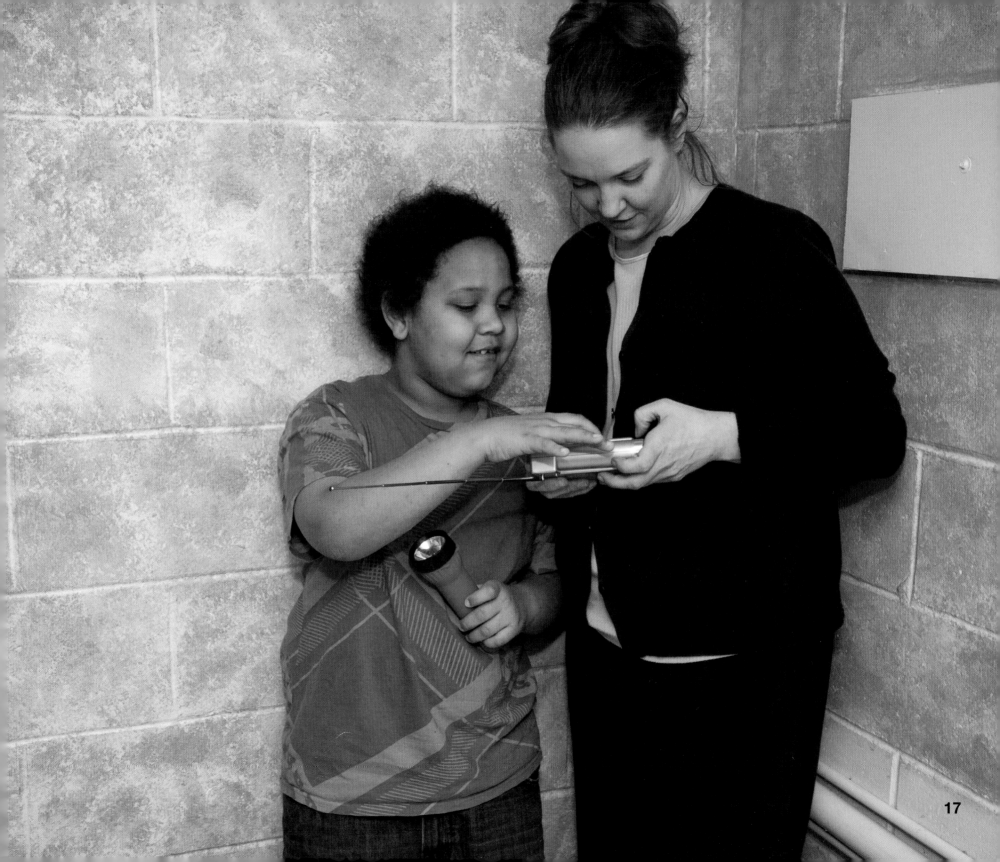

After a Tornado Hits

Tornado damage can show

the tornado's wind speed.

Experts rate the tornado

from one to five on

the Fujita scale.

Strong tornadoes can destroy homes, buildings, and towns. People work together to rebuild after a tornado.

Glossary

air mass — a huge body of air spread out over a large area of land or ocean

damage — harm done to buildings and towns after a storm

destroy — to break something; tornadoes can wipe out everything in their path.

Doppler radar — radar that shows the wind speed and the direction of storms

Fujita scale — a scale from one to five that uses tornado damage to find out how strong a tornado was

funnel — a cone shape with an open top and bottom; tornadoes are often shaped like funnels.

meteorologist — a person who studies and predicts the weather

Tornado Alley — an area of the United States that has hundreds of tornadoes a year

Read More

Doeden, Matt. *Tornadoes.* Pull Ahead Books: Forces of Nature. Minneapolis: Lerner, 2008.

Mezzanotte, Jim. *Tornadoes.* Storms. Milwaukee: Weekly Reader Early Learning Library, 2007.

Wendorff, Anne. *Tornadoes.* Extreme Weather. Minneapolis: Bellwether Media, 2009.

Internet Sites

FactHound offers a safe, fun way to find Internet sites related to this book. All of the sites on FactHound have been researched by our staff.

Here's all you do:

Visit *www.facthound.com*

FactHound will fetch the best sites for you!

Index

Word Count: 156
Grade: 1
Early-Intervention Level: 24